Constitution Translated for Kids

by

Cathy Travis

Oakwood publishing

Oakwood Publishing Books

Oakwood Publishing
P.O. Box 403
Dayton, OH 45409
(937) 298-1998
Find us on the World Wide Web at:
http://www.oakwoodpublishing.com

Published by Oakwood Publishing

2001 copyright

ISBN 1-59165-000-3

9 8 7 6 5 4 3 2 1

Printed and bound in the United States of America.

Acknowledgements:

●●

Cecilia, who inspired me to undertake this endeavor; to Mama Polly, who inspires me always; and to Mama, who made it all possible.

Dedication

For Babycakes, Dobber, Tiger
and Shelby - all of whom I want
to have a clear understanding of
the rights and responsibilities of
democracy

On Democracy.....

"Injustice anywhere is a threat to justice everywhere."
· Dr. Martin Luther King, Jr., letter from the Birmingham jail, published in the <u>Atlantic Monthly</u>, August, 1963

"A government of laws, and not of men."
· John Adams, Novanglus Papers -- <u>Boston Gazette</u>, 1774

"The Constitution is the promise of our independence."
· Hon. Solomon P. Ortiz, Congressional Hispanic Caucus Chair, 1992

"Why has government been instituted at all? Because the passions of men will not conform to the dictates of reason and justice, without restraint."
· Alexander Hamilton, <u>The Federalist Papers</u> [no. II], 1787-1788

"One country, one constitution, one destiny."
· Hon. Daniel Webster, Senate speech, 1837

"[In the Declaration of Independence] is the assertion of the natural right of all to the ballot; for how can 'the consent of the governed' be given if the right to vote be denied?"
· Susan B. Anthony, speech prior to her trial for attempting to vote, 1873

"The basis of our political system is the right of the people to make and to alter their constitutions of government."
· President George Washington, Farewell Address, September 17, 1796

"[Originally] I was not included in 'We the People'.... But through the process of amendment, interpretation and court decision I have finally been included in 'We the People.'"
· Hon. Barbara C. Jordan, Impeachment proceedings of President Richard M. Nixon, July 25, 1974

"No man is above the law and no man is below it; nor do we ask any man's permission when we require him to obey it. Obedience to the law is demanded as a right; not asked as a favor."
· President Theodore Roosevelt, Third Annual Message, December 7, 1903

Table Of Contents

●

A Message to Teachers, Parents, and other Adults:

Childhood years spent wondering how the government works, or what it is, while listening to TV news and hearing crotchety relatives disparage the "govimint," beget apathetic adults. This book is an attempt to make what the Constitution says easier to understand so children will know their rights and protections under the Constitution. While no book can magically end political apathy, it can help teach kids what to expect from their government, its institutions and its leaders.

We are an electorate still very much moved by force of personality. But it is the Constitution that endures, through each President and each Congress, the personalities of our leaders and the social dynamic of our times.

The foundation of all the laws in our country is the U.S. Constitution. No other document or aspect of our federal government supersedes the Constitution, yet precious few people understand that. The language of the times in which it was written, particularly the legalistic language of the late 18th century, makes the message of the Constitution awkward and difficult to understand.

For instance, most hunters know that the Second Amendment gives them the right to own a gun. Yet very few know that the impetus of the amendment was to provide for a national guard. Fewer still know that the word "gun" does not actually appear there.

What usually surprises people the most about the Constitution is the discovery that by casting a vote for their candidate for President of the United States every four years in the general election, they essentially vote for electors (although the results of the 2000 Presidential election in Florida served as a fabulous civics lesson on precisely that).

The Constitution is ever-present in our lives. When the nation was attacked in 2001, Congress (with the Constitutional power to declare war) gave the President (the Commander-in-Chief of the armed forces of the United States) the authority to pursue the attackers militarily.

The text of the Constitution, in this translation, is gender-neutral ... an interesting task, given nearly all states that ratified the Constitution originally granted the right to vote only to white male property owners over 21. The very forward-thinking states (a small number) granted the right to vote to white males who did NOT own property. We have improved on our democracy since then.

This document created the most successful system of government in the last two centuries, despite the human frailties of office holders and citizens ... despite their emotions, doubts, fears, greed, anger, indecision or bad decisions from time to time. The enduring magic of the Constitution is in the ideas this nation represents. Our independence was forged in the belief that our common pursuit of life, liberty and the pursuit of happiness would successfully govern a nation for the ages. The Constitution enshrined that philosophy.

There is no political message here, only the text of the Constitution revised in such a way that it can be easily understood. For those who doubt what the Constitution actually says, the original text of the Constitution, as written and adopted in 1787, appears on the left hand side of the page (complete with Old English spelling and irregular caps), and the translation appears on the right side of the page.

The only message is that the ideas in the Constitution are relatively simple once people understand what they are. By no means is this book a definitive word on the U.S. Constitution. There are plenty of other books about that, not to mention Supreme Court decisions (which are the definitive word on it), and over 200 years of our history. This is just to make the essence of it easier to understand for young people.

There is a glossary of terms in the back, words that may be simple to adults but somewhat confusing to kids. There is also a workbook to guide adults in helping children retain what they are reading by answering questions and engaging in exercises that approximate some of the weighty decisions made in the name of our democracy.

Cathy Travis

Message to Children:

Ever wonder what the adults are talking about when they say things about the government? Or what it means when people say something is constitutional? Here's a way for you to set the adults straight.

When our country got started, there was a group of men called the "Founders." The Founders were people whose families came to this part of the world from Europe almost 100 years before. They liked this place more than Europe and they had a war to be independent.

They wanted to write down the rules and directions for a new and fair kind of government, so they wrote the Constitution. The rules they wrote down have been our directions on how to run the country. Just like we have rules in football, basketball or soccer, we have these rules for running the government.

You may wonder what the rules are that everybody always seems to talk about. So, these are our rules, it is called the U.S. Constitution. It has seven parts called Articles, some longer and harder to understand than others, plus 27 additions to it, called amendments. Some of them are also long.

On the left side of the page are the actual words of the U.S. Constitution from 1787, so if somebody doesn't believe you, you can show them the words used in the real thing. There may still be some hard words in the translation on the right hand side; they are listed in the back to tell you what they mean.

This is a wonderful country, and it is important for everybody to know what the rules are for us. If more people know these rules, our country will be a better place as you understand how to participate in our government. If you know your rights, the Constitution will always work for you.

Help teach the adults what the Constitution actually says.....

Cathy Travis

Text of the United States Constitution (actual)	Translation of the Text of the U.S. Constitution
WE THE PEOPLE of the United States, in Order to form a more perfect Union, establish Justice, insure domestic Tranquility, provide for the common defence, promote the general Welfare, and secure the Blessings of Liberty to ourselves and our Posterity, do ordain and establish this Constitution for the United States of America.	WE THE PEOPLE of the United States – so we can make a country, get along fairly, stay safe, defend ourselves, take care of each other, and make sure we and our children stay free – now write the highest, most supreme law of the United States in this Constitution.

ARTICLE I

ARTICLE I

SECTION 1. All legislative Powers herein granted shall be vested in a Congress of the United States, which shall consist of a Senate and House of Representatives.

SECTION 1. Laws are made by Congress. Congress is made up of a Senate and a House of Representatives.

SECTION 2. The House of Representatives shall be composed of Members chosen every second Year by the People of the several States, and the Electors in each State shall have the Qualifications requisite for Electors of the most numerous Branch of the State Legislature.

SECTION 2. Members of the House of Representatives get elected every two years. The people who get to vote are the same people who get to vote for members of the biggest house of the state legislature (in other words, people who are registered to vote).

No Person shall be a Representative who shall not have attained to the Age of twenty five Years, and been seven Years a Citizen of the United States, and who shall not, when elected, be an Inhabitant of that State in which he shall be chosen.

To get elected to the House, you must be 25 years old, be a citizen of the United States for seven years, and live in the state that elects you.

Representatives and direct Taxes shall be apportioned among the several States which may be included within this Union, according to their respective Numbers, which shall be determined by adding to the whole Number of free Persons, including those bound to Service for a Term of Years, and excluding Indians not taxed, three fifths of all other Persons. The actual Enumeration shall be made within three years after the first Meeting of the Congress of the United States, and within every subse-

[Representatives and taxes were originally based on population which did not count slaves and Indians as full people; Section 2 of the 14th Amendment changed how people are counted]

Representatives in Congress, as well as taxes [this part about taxes was changed by the 16th Amendment], are spread out over the country and are based on the number of people living in the places they represent.

quent Term of ten Years, in such Manner as they shall by Law direct. The number of Representatives shall not exceed one for every thirty Thousand, but each State shall have at Least one Representative; and until such enumeration shall be made, the State of New Hampshire shall be entitled to chuse three, Massachusetts eight, Rhode-Island and Providence Plantations one, Connecticut five, New-York six, New Jersey, four, Pennsylvania eight, Delaware one, Maryland six, Virginia ten, North Carolina five, South Carolina five, and Georgia three.

People in the country get counted every 10 years in a census so we know how many people are in the country, and so we can figure how many people are represented in the House of Representatives, and so we can figure taxes. A certain number of people (originally 30,000; now over 500,000) have their own representative.

For the first Congress, with no census, the division of Representatives in the House was: New Hampshire, three; Massachusetts, eight; Rhode-Island and Providence Plantations, one; Connecticut, five; New-York, six; New Jersey, four; Pennsylvania, eight; Delaware, one; Maryland, six; Virginia, ten; North Carolina, five; South Carolina, five; and Georgia, three.

When vacancies happen in the Representation from any State, the Executive Authority thereof shall issue Writs of Election to fill such Vacancies.

If a Representative leaves office or dies, the Governor of that State sets up another election.

The House of Representatives shall chuse their Speaker and other Officers; and shall have the sole Power of Impeachment.

Representatives get to pick a Speaker and other officers. Only the House of Representatives can vote to start the process for kicking somebody out of office (impeaching them).

SECTION 3. The Senate of the United States shall be composed of two Senators from each State, chosen by the Legislature thereof, for six Years; and each Senator shall have one Vote.

SECTION 3. [Originally, Senators were chosen by the state legislatures, but the 17th Amendment changed it so people in the states voted directly for Senators.]

Immediately after they shall be assembled in Consequence of the first Election, they shall be divided as equally as may be into three Classes. The Seats of the Senators of the first of the second Class at the Expiration of the fourth Year, and of the third Class at the Expiration of the sixth Year, so that one third may be chosen every

The Senate of the United States will have two Senators from each state elected every six years. Each Senator has one vote in the Senate.

After the first election of Senators in the U.S., they will divide themselves into three groups, each picking a term of two, four, and six years for their first

second Year; and if Vacancies happen by Resignation, or otherwise, during the Recess of the Legislature of any State, the Executive thereof may make temporary Appointments until the next Meeting of the Legislature, which shall then fill such Vacancies.

No Person shall be a Senator who shall not have attained to the Age of thirty Years, and been nine Years a Citizen of the United States, and who shall not, when elected, be an Inhabitant of that State for which he shall be chosen.

The Vice President of the United States shall be President of the Senate, but shall have no Vote, unless they be equally divided.

The Senate shall chuse their other Officers, and also a President pro tempore, in the Absence of the Vice President, or when he shall exercise the Office of President of the United States.

The Senate shall have sole Power to try all Impeachments. When sitting for that Purpose, they shall be on Oath or Affirmation. When the President of the United States is tried, the Chief Justice shall preside: And no Person shall be convicted without the Concurrence of two thirds of the Members present.

Judgement in Cases of Impeachment shall not extend further than to removal from Office, and disqualification to hold and enjoy any Office of honor, Trust or Profit under the United States; but the Party convicted shall nevertheless be liable and subject to Indictment, Trial, Judgement and Punishment, according to Law.

term so after that, one-third of the senators are elected every two years.

If a Senator leaves office or dies, the Governor of the State will pick someone to be the Senator until the next election.

To be a Senator, you have to be 30 years old, be a citizen of the United States for nine years, and live in the state that elects you.

The Vice President of the United States will be the President of the Senate, but only gets to vote if there is a tie.

The Senate gets to pick another President of the Senate for the times when the Vice President cannot be there.

The Senate will hold the trials for people the House of Representatives impeaches. If the Senate is trying someone on impeachment (to kick someone out of office), everyone has to swear to tell the truth. If the President of the United States is tried, the Chief Justice of the United States is in charge. But nobody can get kicked out of office unless two-thirds of the Senators present vote for it.

People impeached by Congress cannot be elected or appointed to another office. But if somebody gets impeached and then gets kicked out of office, he or she may still be tried before a jury for any crimes, like the law says.

SECTION 4. The Times, Places and Manner of holding Elections for Senators and Representatives, shall be prescribed in each State by the Legislature thereof; but the Congress may at any time by Law make or alter such Regulations, except as to the Places of chusing Senators.

The Congress shall assemble at least once in every Year, and such Meeting shall be on the first Monday in December, unless they shall by Law appoint a different Day.

SECTION 5. Each House shall be the Judge of the Elections, Returns and Qualifications of its own Members, and a Majority of each shall constitute a Quorum to do Business; but a smaller Number may adjourn from day to day, and may be authorized to compel the Attendance of absent Members, in such manner, and under such Penalties as each House may provide.

Each House may determine the Rules of its Proceedings, punish its Members for disorderly Behaviour, and, with the Concurrence of two thirds, expel a Member.

Each House shall keep a Journal of its Proceedings, and from time to time publish the same, excepting such Parts as may in their Judgment require Secrecy; and the Yeas and Nays of the Members of either House on any question shall, at the Desire of one fifth of those Present, be entered on the Journal.

Neither House, during the Session of Congress, shall, without the Consent of the other, adjourn for more than three days, nor to any other Place than that in which the two Houses shall be sitting.

SECTION 4. The State Legislatures will pick the times and places for elections, but Congress can make laws to change the times and places for Senators and Representatives. [Originally, Congress could not change rules about where Senators were chosen, but the 17th Amendment made that out-of-date.]

The Congress will meet at least once every year, at a regular time [originally, they were to meet on the first Monday in December, but Section 2 of the 20th Amendment changed that to noon on January 3, unless they make a law to move it to another day.]

SECTION 5. The House of Representatives and the Senate are each in charge of the elections and behavior of their Members. Both the House of Representatives and the Senate need most of their Members there to do business. They can make the other Members come to work and punish them if they do not.

Both the House of Representatives and the Senate make their own rules for doing business. They can punish Members for misbehaving, and they can kick out Members if two-thirds of them vote for it.

Both the House of Representatives and the Senate will write down what they say and do in a journal and print it so everybody can read it, unless it is really secret. Votes of individual Representatives or Senators must be written down if 20% of the Members want that.

While Congress is meeting, the House of Representatives or the Senate cannot leave for more than three days, unless they both decide to leave.

SECTION 6. The Senators and Representatives shall receive a Compensation for their Services, to be ascertained by Law, and paid out of the Treasury of the United States. They shall in all Cases, except Treason, Felony and Breach of the Peace, be privileged from Arrest during their Attendance at the Session of their respective Houses, and in going to and returning from the same; and for any Speech or Debate in either House, they shall not be questioned in any other Place.

No Senator or Representative shall, during the Time for which he was elected, be appointed to any civil Office under the Authority of the United States, which shall have been created, or the Emoluments whereof shall have been encreased during such time; and no Person holding any Office under the United States, shall be a Member of either House during his Continuance in Office.

SECTION 7. All Bills for raising Revenue shall originate in the House of Representatives; but the Senate may propose or concur with Amendments as on other Bills.

Every Bill which shall have passed the House of Representatives and the Senate, shall, before it becomes a Law, be presented to the President of the United States; If he approve he shall sign it, but if not he shall return it, with his Objections to that House in which it shall have originated, who shall enter the Objections at large on their Journal, and proceed to reconsider it. If after such Reconsideration two thirds of that House shall agree to pass the Bill, it shall be sent, together with the Objections, to the other House, by which it shall likewise be reconsidered, and if approved by two thirds of that House, it shall become a Law. But in all such Cases the Votes of both Houses shall be determined by yeas and Nays, and the Names of the

SECTION 6. Senators and Representatives will get paid by the government according to the law. Except for treason, stealing, or disturbing the peace, they cannot be arrested while they are at work, or on their way to work, in Congress.

[Congress modified this a little bit in the 27th Amendment, making any change in pay for Congress apply to the next Congress, not the one that voted for it]

No Senator or Representative can be picked for another office in the U.S. Government if that office was created, or if the office got a pay raise, while they were in Congress. No one can serve in Congress and work somewhere else in the government at the same time.

SECTION 7. Any bill raising money (taxes) must begin in the House of Representatives, but the Senate must agree with it, just like any other bill.

When a bill passes both the House and the Senate, the bill goes to the President who must sign it to make it the law. If the President agrees with the bill, the President signs it -- but if the President does not agree with the bill, within 10 days, the President writes down why and sends that letter and the bill back to the House of Representatives or the Senate, wherever the bill got started. When Congress gets the letter and the bill back from the President, the House of Representatives or the Senate puts it all in their journal. Then they talk about it again and vote on it again. If two-thirds of the Representatives and Senators vote for the same bill again, it becomes law. The Representatives and the Senators must have their votes

Persons voting for and against the Bill shall be entered on the Journal of each House respectively. If any Bill shall not be returned by the President within ten Days (Sundays excepted) after it shall have been presented to him, the Same shall be a law, in like Manner as if he had signed it, unless the Congress by their Adjournment prevent its Return, in which Case it shall not be a law.

Every Order, Resolution, or Vote to which the Concurrence of the Senate and House of Representatives may be necessary (except on a question of Adjournment) shall be presented to the President of the United States; and before the Same shall take Effect, shall be approved by him, or being disapproved by him, shall be repassed by two thirds of the Senate and House of Representatives, according to the Rules and Limitations prescribed in the Case of a Bill.

SECTION 8. The Congress shall have Power To lay and collect Taxes, Duties, Imposts and Excises, to pay the Debts and provide for the common Defence and general Welfare of the United States; but all Duties, Imposts and Excises shall be uniform throughout the United States;

To borrow Money on the credit of the United States;

To regulate Commerce with foreign Nations, and among the several States, and with the Indian Tribes;

To establish a uniform Rule of Naturalization, and uniform Laws on the subject of Bankruptcies throughout the United States;

To coin Money, regulate the Value thereof, and of foreign Coin, and fix the Standard of Weights and Measures;

written down on this vote in their journal. If the President does not sign the bill, or does not send the bill back to Congress in 10 days (not counting Sundays), then it becomes law, unless Congress officially leaves to go home (adjourns).

Each law passed by the House of Representatives and the Senate must be signed by the President -- or the President must agree with it -- and the ones the President does not agree with (those that get "vetoed") must be passed by two-thirds of the House of Representatives and the Senate before it can be the law.

SECTION 8. Congress has the job of raising and spending money to take care of the nation, but all taxes raised must be the same for all the States.

Other jobs of Congress are:

To borrow money;

To make rules for how people do business, including buying and selling things with people in other countries, among the states, and with Native Americans;

To decide on fair rules for letting people become citizens -- and rules for bankruptcies in all the States;

To print paper money and make coins, and to figure out how much it will be worth; to figure the worth of money from other countries; and to decide on

Original	Plain Language
	a system of weights and measures;
To provide for the Punishment of counterfeiting the Securities and current Coin of the United States;	To punish people who copy money or bonds of the United States;
To establish Post Offices and post Roads;	To build post offices and roads;
To promote the Progress of Science and useful Arts, by securing for limited Times to Authors and Inventors the exclusive Right to their respective Writings and Discoveries;	To promote science and the arts by giving copyrights to writers and inventors for things they write and discover;
To constitute Tribunals inferior to the supreme Court;	To keep a system of courts around the country to support the Supreme Court;
To define and punish Piracies and Felonies committed on the high Seas, and Offenses against the Law of Nations;	To make laws about what people can and cannot do on the oceans;
To declare War, grant Letters of Marque and Reprisal, and make Rules concerning Captures on Land and Water;	To make war, to allow private boats and vessels to catch and arrest enemy ships, and to make rules about taking prisoners on the land and on the water;
To raise and support Armies, but no Appropriation of money to that Use shall be for a longer Term than two Years;To provide and maintain a Navy;	To build an army and to pay for it -- but money for the army can only be given for, at the most, two years at a time;
To provide and maintain a Navy	To build a Navy and to pay for it;
To make Rules for the Government and Regulation of the land and naval Forces;	To make all the rules for the government and the Army and the Navy;
To provide for calling forth the Militia to execute the Laws of the Union, suppress Insurrections and repel Invasions;	To make rules for calling the state National Guards to force people to obey the law, stop riots and to fight attackers;
To provide for organizing, arming, and disciplining, the Militia, and for governing such Part of them as may be employed in the Service of the United States, reserving to the States respectively, the Appointment of the Officers, and the Authority of training the Militia according to the discipline pre-	To organize the States' National Guards and to give them guns and equipment – and to be in charge of them if they are working for the United States. But the states get to be in charge of the training Congress wants, and the states each get to pick the officers of the National Guard in their state;

scribed by Congress;

To exercise exclusive Legislation in all Cases whatsoever, over such District (not exceeding ten Miles square) as may, by Cession of particular States, and the Acceptance of Congress, become the Seat of the Government of the United States, and to exercise like Authority over all Places purchased by the Consent of the Legislature of the State in which the Same shall be, for the Erection of Forts, Magazines, Arsenals, dock-Yards, and other needful Buildings; --- And

To be in charge of a place, no bigger than 10 square miles, a place given by the states and accepted by Congress, which will be the seat of the federal government. [This is present-day Washington, D.C.] Congress will be in charge of all the places bought and run by the government, AND

To make all Laws which shall be necessary and proper for carrying into Execution the foregoing Powers, and all other Powers vested by this Constitution in the Government of the United States, or in any Department or Officer thereof.

To make all the laws Congress needs to enforce the powers given to Congress by this Constitution.

SECTION 9. The Migration or Importation of such Persons as any of the States now existing shall think proper to admit, shall not be prohibited by the Congress prior to the Year one thousand eight hundred and eight, but a Tax or duty may be imposed on such Importation, not exceeding ten dollars for each Person.

SECTION 9. The slave trade cannot be banned by Congress until at least 1808, but a tax of up to $10 can be put on imported slaves.

[Slavery was banned by the 13th Amendment.]

The Privilege of the Writ of Habeas Corpus shall not be suspended, unless when in Cases of Rebellion or Invasion the public Safety may require it.

Rights of people in jail to make the government show why they are in jail can be taken away only if there is a rebellion, or if the United States is invaded by a foreign power.

No Bill of Attainder or ex post facto Law shall be passed.

Congress cannot pass a law to declare someone guilty of a crime. Criminal laws passed by Congress can be applied only from the time they are passed.

No Capitation, or other direct, Tax shall be laid, unless in Proportion to the Census or Enumeration herein before directed to be taken.	Congress must tax according to the number of citizens there are in the country, according to the Census. [The 16th Amendment changed this so Congress could charge and collect taxes any way they wanted.]
No Tax or Duty shall be laid on Articles exported from any State.	Congress cannot tax things sold from one state to another state.
No Preference shall be given by any Regulation of Commerce or Revenue to the Ports of one State over those of another: nor shall Vessels bound to, or from, one State, be obliged to enter, clear, or pay Duties in another.	Congress cannot prefer one port over another, and no ships from one state can get taxed for using another state's port.
No Money shall be drawn from the Treasury, but in Consequence of Appropriations made by Law; and a regular Statement and Account of the Receipts and Expenditures of all public Money shall be published from time to time.	No money can be spent without Congress passing an Appropriations law, and they must publish a regular Statement of the Treasury Account from time to time.
No Title of Nobility shall be granted by the United States: And no Person holding any Office of Profit or Trust under them, shall, without the Consent of the Congress, accept of any present, Emolument, Office, or Title, of any kind whatever, from any King, Prince, or foreign State.	Congress cannot give anyone any title of nobility (King, Queen, Prince, Lord, etc.), and no officer of the United States can accept any title, office or payment of any kind from any other country.
SECTION 10. No State shall enter into any Treaty, Alliance, or Confederation; grant Letters of Marque and Reprisal; coin Money; emit Bills of Credit; make any Thing but gold and silver Coin a Tender in Payment of Debts, pass any Bill of Attainder, ex post facto Law, or Law impairing the Obligation of Contracts, or grant any Title of Nobility.	SECTION 10. No state can ally with another country; make war; make their own money; allow private boats and vessels to catch and arrest enemy ships; or issue their own bills for credit. States must make only silver and gold to pay for things. States cannot pass any law to disgrace people accused of dishonor. States cannot pass a law that goes back in time. Laws can be applied only after they are passed. States cannot pass a law that messes up contracts already made. States may not give people a title of nobility.

No State shall, without the Consent of the Congress, lay any Imposts or duties on Imports or Exports, except what may be absolutely necessary for executing it's inspection Laws: and the net Produce of all Duties and Imposts, laid by any State on Imports or Exports, shall be for the Use of the Treasury of the United States; and all such Laws shall be subject to the Revision and Controul of the Congress.

No State shall, without the Consent of Congress, lay any Duty of Tonnage, keep Troops, or Ships of War in time of Peace, enter into any Agreement or Compact with another State, or with a foreign Power, or engage in War, unless actually invaded, or in such imminent Danger as will not admit of delay.

States must have the permission of Congress to charge money for the buying and selling of things that come into the country and things sold outside of the country. If states pass laws to charge money for things that come into and go out of the country, all the money collected will go to the United States Treasury. Congress can make laws to change or control these state laws.

States must have Congress' permission to keep armies, or warships during peacetime. States will need Congress' permission to join forces with another state or with a foreign power, or to make war, unless they are invaded and the United States troops cannot get there in time to help.

ARTICLE. II.

SECTION 1. The executive Power shall be vested in a President of the United States of America. He shall hold his Office during the Term of four Years, and, together with the Vice President, chosen for the same Term, be elected, as follows:

Each State shall appoint, in such Manner as the Legislature thereof may direct, a Number of Electors, equal to the whole Number of Senators and Representatives to which the State may be entitled in the Congress: but no Senator or Representative, or Person holding an Office of Trust or Profit under the United States, shall be appointed an Elector.

The Electors shall meet in their respective States, and vote by Ballot for two Persons, of whom one at least shall not be an Inhabitant of the same State with themselves. And they shall make a List of all the Persons voted for, and of the Number of Votes for each; which List they shall sign and certify, and transmit sealed to the Seat of the Government of the United States, directed to the President of the Senate. The President of the Senate shall, in the Presence of the Senate and House of Representatives, open all the Certificates, and the Votes shall then be counted. The Person having the greatest Number of Votes shall be the President, if such Number be a Majority of the whole Number of Electors appointed; and if there be more than one who have such Majority, and have an equal Number of Votes, then the House of Representatives shall immediately chuse by Ballot one of them for President; and if no Person have a majority, then from the five highest on the List the said House shall in like

ARTICLE II

SECTION 1. The leader of the country will be the President of the United States. The President will be elected every four years, along with a Vice President, like this:

The legislature of each state decides how that state will name a number of people called "Electors." The number of electors will equal the number of Representatives and Senators of that State -- but Senators, Representatives, or other government officers cannot be electors. (If a state has four Representatives and two Senators, it has six electors in what is now known as the Electoral College.)

The electors meet in their states and vote for two people. At least one person for whom they vote cannot live in that elector's state. The Electors will make a list of all the people they voted for, and how many votes each person got. Then they sign and certify the list, and send it to the President of the Senate in the seat of the United States Government (in Washington, D.C.). The President of the Senate opens all the States' certificates in front of the Representatives and Senators, and then the votes are counted. The person with the majority of electors' votes will be the President. If more than one person has the same number of electors' votes, the Representatives will immediately choose one of them by a vote. If nobody has a majority, then the Representatives will choose a President from among the five people who got the most electors' votes. But if the Representatives have to choose a President like this, the vote will be taken by States, and each state has only one vote. At least two-thirds of the Representatives must be present to

Manner chuse the President. But in chusing the President, the Votes shall be taken by States, the Representation from each State having one Vote; A quorum for this Purpose shall consist of a Member or Members from two-thirds of the States, and a Majority of all the States shall be necessary to a Choice. In every Case, after the Choice of the President, the Person having the greatest Number of Votes of the Electors shall be the Vice President. But if there should remain two or more who have equal Votes, the Senate shall chuse from them by Ballot the Vice President.

choose a President like this. If the President has to be chosen like this, the person with the next most electors' votes will be the Vice President. If there is a tie, the Senators vote for the Vice President.

[The 12th Amendment and the 23rd Amendment changed this process]

The Congress may determine the Time of chusing the Electors, and the Day on which they shall give their Votes; which Day shall be the same throughout the United States.

Congress picks the time of choosing of electors, and the day they vote. It will be the same day in all States.

No Person except a natural born Citizen, or a Citizen of the United States, at the time of the Adoption of this Constitution, shall be eligible to the Office of President; neither shall any person be eligible to that Office who shall not have attained to the Age of thirty-five Years, and been fourteen Years a Resident within the United States.

The President must be born a United States citizen, be 35 years old, and have lived in the United States for 14 years.

In Case of the Removal of the President from Office, or of his Death, Resignation, or Inability to discharge the Powers and Duties of the said Office, the Same shall devolve on the Vice President, and the Congress may by Law provide for the Case of Removal, Death, Resignation or Inability, both of the President and Vice President, declaring what Officer shall then act as President, and such Officer shall act accordingly, until the

If the President dies, leaves office, is kicked out of office, or is unable to do the job -- the duties of President fall to the Vice President. Congress will decide how to handle things if the President or Vice President dies, leaves office, gets kicked out of office, or is unable to do their jobs. Congress will figure out which officer will act as President if the elected President or Vice President is unable to do their job, until the elected President or Vice

Disability be removed, or a President shall be elected.

The President shall, at stated Times, receive for his Services, a Compensation, which shall neither be increased nor diminished during the Period for which he shall have been elected, and he shall not receive within that period any other Emolument from the United States, or any of them.

Before he enter on the Execution of his Office, he shall take the following Oath or Affirmation: "I do solemnly swear (or affirm) that I will faithfully execute the Office of President of the United States, and will to the best of my Ability, preserve, protect and defend the Constitution of the United States."

SECTION 2. The President shall be the Commander in Chief of the Army and Navy of the United States, and of the Militia of the several States, when called into the actual service of the United States; he may require the Opinion, in writing, of the principal Officer in each of the executive Departments, upon any Subject relating to the Duties of their respective Offices, and he shall have Power to grant Reprieves and Pardons for Offenses against the United States, except in Cases of Impeachment.

He shall have Power, by and with the Advice and Consent of the Senate, to make Treaties, provided two-thirds of the Senators present concur; and he shall nominate, and by and with the Advice and Consent of the Senate, shall appoint Ambassadors, other public Ministers and Consuls, Judges of the supreme Court, and all other

President can do their job again, or until another President is elected. [This got more specific with the 25th Amendment]

The President will get paid for serving as President, and the pay cannot go up or down while that person serves as President. The President cannot get paid anything but salary from the United States while President. The President cannot get money from any State.

When the President takes office, this is the oath: "I do solemnly swear (or affirm) that I will faithfully execute the Office of President of the United States, and will to the best of my ability, preserve, protect, and defend the Constitution of the United States."

SECTION 2. The President is the Commander-in-Chief, in charge of the Army, Navy and all the armed forces of the United States. The President is also in charge of the National Guard of the States if the Guard is working for the United States. The President may get the officers of the executive departments to write down their ideas about anything of which they are in charge. The President can pardon people for crimes against the United States, except when those people get impeached by the House of Representatives and found guilty by the Senate.

The President has the power to make treaties, with the advice and permission of two thirds of the Senators present. The President will also appoint, with the advice and permission of two thirds of the Senators, Ambassadors (U.S. representatives in other countries), Supreme Court Judges, and other U.S. officers. Congress must

Officers of the United States, whose Appointments are not herein otherwise provided for, and which shall be established by Law: but the Congress may by Law vest the Appointment of such inferior Officers, as they think proper, in the President alone, in the Courts of Law, or in the Heads of Departments.

The President shall have Power to fill up all Vacancies that may happen during the Recess of the Senate, by granting Commissions which shall expire at the End of their next Session.

SECTION 3. He shall from time to time give to the Congress Information of the State of the Union, and recommend to their Consideration such Measures as he shall judge necessary and expedient; he may, on extraordinary Occasions, convene both Houses, or either of them, and in Case of Disagreement between them, with Respect to the Time of Adjournment, he may adjourn them to such Time as he shall think proper; he shall receive Ambassadors and other public Ministers; he shall take Care that the Laws be faithfully executed, and shall Commission all the Officers of the United States.

SECTION 4. The President, Vice President and all civil Officers of the United States, shall be removed from Office on Impeachment for, and Conviction of, Treason, Bribery, or other high Crimes and Misdemeanors.

approve the President's treaties with a two-thirds vote of Senators present. Congress will decide how other appointments will be handled. Congress can let the President, the courts, or Department heads appoint other officers as they see fit.

If Congress is not in session, the President can fill vacancies whose term ends at the end of the next session of Congress.

SECTION 3. The President will tell Congress how the country is doing in a "State of the Union" speech from time to time. The President will also give Congress ideas about how to get things done; and the President can meet with Congress anytime it is really important. If the Congress cannot agree on when Congress is finished working for the year, the President can dismiss them until a time the President thinks is fair. The President will welcome Ambassadors or government representatives from other countries; the President is in charge of making sure that the laws are carried out fairly; and the President empowers all the officers of the United States.

SECTION 4. The President, the Vice President, and other officers of the United States, can be kicked out of office (impeached) if they are found guilty of double-crossing (betraying) the country, offering people money or getting money to do something dishonest, or other really big crimes.

ARTICLE III

SECTION 1.

The judicial Power of the United States, shall be vested in one supreme Court, and in such inferior Courts as the Congress may from time to time ordain and establish. The Judges, both of the supreme and inferior Courts, shall hold their Offices during good Behaviour, and shall, at stated Times, receive for their Services, a Compensation, which shall not be diminished during their Continuance in Office.

SECTION 2.

The judicial Power shall extend to all Cases, in Law and Equity, arising under this Constitution, the Laws of the United States, and Treaties made, or which shall be made, under their Authority; -- to all Cases affecting Ambassadors, other public Ministers and Consuls; -- to all Cases of admiralty and maritime Jurisdiction; -- to Controversies to which the United States shall be a Party; -- to Controversies between two or more States; -- between a State and Citizens of another State; -- between Citizens of different States, -- between Citizens of the same State claiming Lands under Grants of different States, and between a State, or the Citizens thereof, and foreign States, Citizens or Subjects.

In all Cases affecting Ambassadors, other public Ministers and Consuls, and those in which a State shall be Party, the supreme Court shall have original Jurisdiction. In all the other Cases before mentioned, the supreme Court shall have appellate Jurisdiction, both as to Law and Fact, with such Exceptions, and under such Regulations as the Congress shall make.

ARTICLE III

SECTION 1.

All the judicial power of the United States, including the courts of law and justice, will be headed by one Supreme Court. Congress can set up other courts as we need them. The Judges on the Supreme Court and the other courts under them can stay judges all their lives if they obey all the laws. The money Judges get paid for their service cannot be cut during their time as a Judge.

SECTION 2.

The judges of the courts have the power to decide any case that involves or questions: the Constitution, laws of the United States, or a treaty signed by the United States. Courts will also decide any case that involves Ambassadors or foreign ministers from other countries. They have the final say on cases that happen on the oceans. They decide: arguments when the United States is involved, cases between two or more states, cases between a state and somebody from another country, cases between citizens of different states, cases between citizens of the same state when different states give them the same land, and to all cases between a state, the citizens in that state, and other countries and their citizens.

[This got changed by the 11th Amendment.]

If an Ambassador or Minister from another country, or if a state is involved, the Supreme Court can hear the case first. In all the other cases, the smaller courts will hear the cases first, and the loser can appeal their case. The Supreme Court is the final authority. The Supreme Court can look at both the law and the facts of each case, with the rules Congress has passed.

The Trial of all Crimes, except in Cases of Impeachment; shall be by Jury; and such Trial shall be held in the State where the said Crimes shall have been committed; but when not committed within any State, the Trial shall be at such Place or Places as the Congress may by Law have directed.

Trial for all federal crimes, except kicking people out of government (impeaching them), will be in front of a jury. The trial will be held in the same state where the crime was committed.

If the crime was not committed in a State, Congress can decide by law where to hold the trial.

SECTION 3. Treason against the United States, shall consist only in levying War against them, or in adhering to their Enemies, giving them Aid and Comfort. No Person shall be convicted of Treason unless on the Testimony of two Witnesses to the same overt Act, or on Confession in open Court.

SECTION 3. Treason, or betraying the United States, is making war against the United States, or being loyal to an enemy of the United States, or giving that enemy help or comfort. Nobody can be found guilty of treason unless two people describe the same obvious act of treason in open court, or unless the accused person says in open court that she/he did it.

The Congress shall have Power to declare the Punishment of Treason, but no Attainder of Treason shall work Corruption of Blood, or Forfeiture except during the Life of the Person attainted.

Congress decides how to punish treason. If someone is guilty of treason, their family cannot be punished. The disgrace of the traitor, and any fines they owe, will go with them to their death, but not past that.

ARTICLE IV.

SECTION 1. Full Faith and Credit shall be given in each State to the public Acts, Records, and judicial Proceedings of every other State; And the Congress may by general Laws prescribe the Manner in which such Acts, Records and Proceedings shall be proved and the Effect thereof.

SECTION 2. The Citizens of each State shall be entitled to all Privileges and Immunities of Citizens in the several States.

A Person charged in any State with Treason, Felony, or other Crime, who shall flee from Justice, and be found in another State, shall on Demand of the executive Authority of the State from which he fled, be delivered up, to be removed to the State having Jurisdiction of the Crime.

No Person held to Service or Labour in one State, under the Laws thereof, escaping into another, shall, in Consequence of any Law or Regulation therein, be discharged from such Service or Labour but shall be delivered up on Claim of the Party to whom such Service or Labour may be due.

SECTION 3. New States may be admitted by the Congress into this Union; but no new State shall be formed or erected within the Jurisdiction of any other State; nor any State be formed by the Junction of two or more States, or Parts of States, without the Consent of the Legislatures of the States concerned as well as of the Congress.

The Congress shall have Power to dispose of and make all needful Rules and Regulations respecting the Territory or other Property belonging to the United States; and nothing in this Constitution

ARTICLE IV

SECTION 1. Each State will honor every other States' public acts, their records, and their legal reports. The Congress will make laws to decide how to check on such acts, records, and reports. Congress will decide how to test these records and how effective they are.

SECTION 2. Citizens of each State will have all the advantages and protection of citizens in the other states.

If somebody is charged with a crime in one state, then runs from the police to another state, the Governor of the state in which the crime was committed can demand the return of that person, and the other state must obey.

A slave in one state who escapes to a state where slavery is outlawed, will be returned to the slave owner upon their request. [The 13th Amendment outlawed slavery, making this part of the Constitution outdated.]

SECTION 3. Congress can let new states into the Union, but no states can be formed inside another State. States cannot be made of two or more States, or parts of States, unless both the State legislatures of those States and Congress agree to it.

Congress has the power to make rules and laws for lands and other property of the United States. Nothing in the Constitution can be used to influence any claims of the United States or any State.

shall be so construed as to Prejudice any claims of the United States, or of any particular State.

SECTION 4. The United States shall guarantee to every State in this Union a Republican Form of Government, and shall protect each of them against Invasion; and on Application of the Legislature, or of the Executive (when the Legislature cannot be convened) against domestic Violence.

SECTION 4. The United States will guarantee every state a government elected by the citizens of that state, and it will protect the States from attack. The United States will also protect the states from local fighting, or riots, if the State legislatures ask for it. The Governor can ask for this protection if the legislature of that state is not meeting.

ARTICLE V

The Congress, whenever two thirds of both Houses shall deem it necessary, shall propose Amendments to this Constitution, or, on the Application of the Legislatures of two thirds of the several States, shall call a Convention for proposing Amendments, which, in either Case, shall be valid to all Intents and Purposes, as Part of this Constitution, when ratified by the Legislatures of three fourths of the several States, or by Conventions in three fourths thereof, as the one or the other Mode of Ratification may be proposed by the Congress; Provided that no Amendment which may be made prior to the Year One thousand eight hundred and eight shall in any Manner affect the first and fourth Clauses in the Ninth Section of the first Article; and that no State, without its Consent, shall be deprived of it's equal Suffrage in the Senate.

ARTICLE V

Amendments, or changes, to this Constitution can be offered two ways: 1. Congress can propose an amendment (it takes two-thirds of the Representatives and Senators to do that). 2. Legislatures of two-thirds of the States can call a big meeting called a Constitutional Convention.

Either way, the amendments will be officially part of the Constitution when three-fourths of the State legislatures approve them. Congress may suggest another way to approve them. No amendment made before the year 1808 can affect the slave trade or taxation. No State, without that state's permission, can go without its right to vote in the Senate.

ARTICLE VI

All Debts contracted and Engagements entered into, before the Adoption of this Constitution, shall be as valid against the United States under this Constitution, as under the Confederation.

This Constitution, and the Laws of the United States which shall be made in Pursuance thereof; and all Treaties made, or which shall be made, under the Authority of the United States, shall be the supreme Law of the Land; and the Judges in every State shall be bound thereby, any Thing in the Constitution or Laws of any State to the Contrary notwithstanding.

The Senators and Representatives before mentioned, and the Members of the several State Legislatures, and all executive and judicial Officers, both of the United States and of the several States, shall be bound by Oath or Affirmation, to support this Constitution; but no religious Test shall ever be required as a Qualification to any Office or public Trust under the United States.

ARTICLE VI

All debts and promises made by the United States before the approval of this Constitution will still be enforced under this Constitution.

This Constitution, the laws of the United States, and the treaties of the United States are the absolute law of the land -- and all judges must honor them, despite anything different in State Constitutions or State laws.

All Senators, Representatives, Members of State Legislatures, executive and judicial officers, both of the United States and in the states themselves, are bound by their word to support this Constitution. No religious test can ever be used in order to serve in public office.

ARTICLE VII

The Ratification of the Conventions of nine States, shall be sufficient for the Establishment of this Constitution between the States so ratifying the Same.

[sic] done in Convention by the Unanimous Consent of the States present the Seventeenth Day of September in the Year of our Lord one thousand seven hundred and Eighty seven and of the Independence of the United States of America the Twelfth. IN WITNESS whereof We have hereunto subscribed our names,

Go. WASHINGTON President and deputy from Virginia

[Signed also by the deputies of twelve States.]

New Hampshire: John Langdon, Nicholas Gilman

Massachusetts: Nathaniel Gorham, Rufus King

Connecticut: Wm. Saml. Johnson, Roger Sherman

New York: Alexander Hamilton

New Jersey: Wil: Livingston, David Brearley,Wm. Paterson, Jona: Dayton

Pennsylvania: B Franklin, Thomas Mifflin, Robt. Morris, Geo. Clymer, Thos. FitzSimons
Jared Ingersol, James Wilson, Gouv Morris

Delaware: Geo: Read, Gunning Bedford jun, John Dickinson, Richard Bassett, Jaco: Broom

Maryland: James McHenry, Dan of St Thos. Jenifer, Danl Carroll

Virginia: John Blair, James Madison Jr.,

North Carolina: Wm. Blount, Richd. Dobbs Spaight, Hu Williamson

South Carolina: J. Rutledge

ARTICLE VII

The approval of the Constitutional meetings in nine States will be enough to approve the creation of this Constitution between the States.

This agreement is made unanimously by the States present on September 17, 1787; twelve years after becoming Independent.

To witness this document, we now sign our names,

== Original signers in left column ==

AMENDMENTS TO THE UNITED STATES CONSTITUTION, PROPOSED BY CONGRESS, AND RATIFIED BY THE LEGISLATURES OF THE SEVERAL STATES, PURSUANT TO THE FIFTH ARTICLE OF THE ORIGINAL CONSTITUTION

AMENDMENTS TO THE UNITED STATES CONSTITUTION, SUGGESTED BY CONGRESS, AND APPROVED BY THE STATES, LIKE THE FIFTH ARTICLE OF THE ORIGINAL CONSTITUTION SAYS

[The first 10 Amendments are also known as "The Bill of Rights"]

AMENDMENT I.

Congress shall make no law respecting an establishment of religion, or prohibiting the free exercise thereof; or abridging the freedom of speech, or of the press; or the right of the people peaceably to assemble, and to petition the Government for a redress of grievances.

AMENDMENT 1 (Dec. 15, 1791)

Congress cannot make any law to create a government church, to keep people from practicing any religion they please (or not), to keep people from writing or saying what is on their minds, to keep people from getting together peacefully, or to keep people from asking the government to hear their complaints.

AMENDMENT II.

A well regulated Militia, being necessary to the security of a free State, the right of the people to keep and bear Arms, shall not be infringed.

AMENDMENT 2 (Dec. 15, 1791)

Since we need a National Guard to secure the country, citizens have the right to own firearms (guns).

AMENDMENT III.

No Soldier shall, in time of peace be quartered in any house, without the consent of the Owner, nor in time of war, but in a manner to be prescribed by law.

AMENDMENT 3 (Dec. 15, 1791)

In peacetime, citizens do not have to let soldiers stay in their house. If there is a war, citizens would not have to let soldiers stay in their house unless there was a law to describe how it should happen.

AMENDMENT IV.

The right of the people to be secure in their persons, houses, papers, and effects, against unreasonable searches and seizures, shall not be violated, and no Warrants shall issue, but upon probable cause, supported by Oath or affirmation, and particularly describing the place to be searched, and the persons or things to be seized.

AMENDMENT 4 (Dec. 15, 1791)

The personal property of people is safe from government intrusion. People, and their houses, papers and other things they own, are protected from the police taking their property or looking at their property without a warrant. If there is a need to search or take property, a Judge must issue a warrant for a very good reason, supported by an oath, and the warrant must describe what is being looked at and what is being taken.

AMENDMENT V.

No person shall be held to answer for a

AMENDMENT 5 (Dec. 15, 1791)

No one can be made to defend them-

capital, or otherwise infamous crime, unless on a presentment or indictment of a Grand Jury, except in cases arising in the land or naval forces, or in the Militia, when in actual service in time of War or public danger; nor shall any person be subject for the same offence to be twice put in jeopardy of life or limb, nor shall be compelled in any criminal case to be a witness against himself, nor be deprived of life, liberty, or property, without due process of law; nor shall private property be taken for public use without just compensation.

selves against a crime the government says he/she committed under federal law unless a group of people (grand jury) agrees that the charge is real, and then that person is officially accused. Cases involving the armed forces or the National Guard are exceptions during wartime. No one can be held responsible for the same crime more than once. No one can be made to testify against himself or herself, and the government cannot take away anyone's life, freedom, or property without applying the law. Private property cannot be taken for public use without a fair payment.

AMENDMENT VI.

In all criminal prosecutions, the accused shall enjoy the right to a speedy and public trial, by an impartial jury of the State and district wherein the crime shall have been committed; which district shall have been previously ascertained by law, and to be informed of the nature and cause of the accusation; to be confronted with the witnesses against him; to have compulsory process for obtaining witnesses in his favor, and to have the assistance of counsel for his defence.

AMENDMENT 6 (Dec. 15, 1791)

In criminal trials, anyone blamed for a crime will enjoy the right to a quick, public trial; decided by an open-minded jury; in the general place (district) where the crime was committed -- these places will be determined by law. Anyone blamed for crimes must be told what crime they are accused of and why they are being blamed. The person blamed for a crime has the right to face the witnesses against him or her, to have a way to bring forward witnesses on his or her side in court, and to have a lawyer for his or her defense.

AMENDMENT VII.

In Suits at common law, where the value in controversy shall exceed twenty dollars, the right of trial by jury shall be preserved, and no fact tried by a jury shall be otherwise re-examined in any Court of the United States, than according to the rules of the common law.

AMENDMENT 7 (Dec. 15, 1791)

In federal cases where somebody sues someone for more than $20, and when the case comes from old laws before the Constitution, the people get to have a trial by jury. No fact examined by a jury can be re-examined in any federal court, except according to the current rules.

AMENDMENT VIII.

Excessive bail shall not be required, nor excessive fines imposed, nor cruel and unusual punishments inflicted.

AMENDMENT 8 (Dec. 15, 1791)

Anyone accused of a federal crime will not be required to pay bail that is out of proportion to the crime. Fines (money) charged to punish criminals must be reasonable, and any other punishment must not be cruel or unusual.

AMENDMENT IX.

The enumeration in the Constitution of certain rights shall not be construed to deny or disparage others retained by the people.

AMENDMENT X.

The powers not delegated to the United States by the Constitution, nor prohibited by it to the States, are reserved to the States respectively, or to the people.

AMENDMENT XI.

The Judicial power of the United States shall not be construed to extend to any suit in law or equity, commenced or prosecuted against one of the United States by Citizens of another State, or by Citizens or Subjects of any Foreign State.

AMENDMENT XII.

The Electors shall meet in their respective states, and vote by ballot for President and Vice-President, one of whom, at least, shall not be an inhabitant of the same state with themselves; they shall name in their ballots the person voted for as President, and in distinct ballots the person voted for as Vice-President, and they shall make distinct lists of all persons voted for as President, and of all persons voted for as Vice-President, and of the number of votes for each, which lists they shall sign and certify, and transmit sealed to the seat of the government of the United States, directed to the President of the Senate; -- The President of the Senate shall, in the presence of the Senate and House of Representatives, open all the certificates and the votes shall then be counted; -- The person having the greatest number of votes for President, shall be the President, if such number be a majority of the whole number of Electors appointed; and if no person have such majority, then from the persons having the highest numbers not exceeding three on the list of those voted for as President, the

AMENDMENT 9 (Dec. 15, 1791)

Just because some rights are listed in the Constitution does not mean that the people do not have other rights.

AMENDMENT 10 (Dec. 15, 1791)

The powers not given to the United States by the Constitution, or denied by it to the States, belong to the States, or to the people themselves.

AMENDMENT 11 (Feb. 7, 1795)

No one can use the power of the Courts against a state unless that person lives in that state. Citizens of another county cannot use the courts to sue any of the States.

AMENDMENT 12 (June 15, 1804)

The Electors will meet in their home States and vote for the President and the Vice President, using a ballot. Electors cannot vote for the President or the Vice President if they are both from the same state as the Elector. On the ballots, the electors must clearly mark their choice for President, and their choice for Vice President. Then the electors will make clear and separate lists of all the people voted for as President, and all the people voted for as Vice President, including how many votes each candidate got. The Electors will sign and approve each list, then they seal the list and send it to the seat of Government (Washington, D.C.), to the attention of the President of the Senate. The President of the Senate opens it in front of the House of Representatives and the Senate, and counts all the votes. The person who has a majority of Electoral votes will be the President.

If no candidate gets a majority of Electoral votes, then the House of Representatives will pick the President, by ballot, from the three

House of Representatives shall choose immediately, by ballot, the President. But in choosing the President, the votes shall be taken by states, the representation from each state having one vote; a quorum for this purpose shall consist of a member or members from two-thirds of the states, and a majority of all the states shall be necessary to a choice. And if the House of Representatives shall not choose a President whenever the right of choice shall devolve upon them, before the fourth day of March next following, then the Vice-President shall act as President, as in the case of the death or other constitutional disability of the President. The person having the greatest number of votes as Vice-President, shall be the Vice-President, if such number be a majority of the whole number of Electors appointed, and if no person have a majority, then from the two highest numbers on the list, the Senate shall choose the Vice-President; a quorum for the purpose shall consist of two-thirds of the whole number of Senators, and a majority of the whole number shall be necessary to a choice. But no person constitutionally ineligible to the office of President shall be eligible to that of Vice-President of the United States.

Presidential candidates who got the most Electoral votes. If this happens, the vote will be taken by States. The delegation (all the Representatives from a state) of each state will have only one vote. A quorum (the least amount of people needed to make a decision) will be at least one member from two-thirds of the States participating. A majority (50% + 1) of all the states will be required to make this decision. If the Representatives fool around and do not make a decision before March 4 of the next year, then the Vice President will be the President, just like if the President were to die or else be unable to serve. [The 20th Amendment added a little more about this.]

The person with the majority of Electoral votes for Vice-President will be the Vice President. If no candidate gets a majority of Electoral votes, then the Senate will pick the Vice-President, by ballot, from the two Vice-Presidential candidates who got the most Electoral votes. At least two-thirds of the Senators are needed to make this decision; and a majority (50% + one) of the Senate will be required to make the final choice. The Constitutional guidelines for the President are the same for the Vice President.

AMENDMENT XIII.

SECTION 1. Neither slavery nor involuntary servitude, except as a punishment for crime whereof the party shall have been duly convicted, shall exist within the United States, or any place subject to their jurisdiction.

SECTION 2. Congress shall have power to enforce this article by appropriate legislation.

AMENDMENT XIV.

SECTION 1. All persons born or naturalized in the United States and subject to the jurisdiction thereof, are citizens of the United States and of the State wherein they reside. No State shall make or enforce any law which

AMENDMENT 13 (Dec. 6, 1865)

SECTION 1. Slavery no longer exists in the United States or any place the United States controls. No one is forced to work for anyone else for no pay, except as punishment for a crime in which the criminal has been convicted by a court of law.

SECTION 2. Congress has the power to enforce this amendment with laws.

AMENDMENT 14 (July 9, 1868)

SECTION 1. Anyone born in the United States, or given citizenship by the United States, is a citizen of the United States and citizens of the state where they live. States cannot make or enforce any laws that limit the rewards

shall abridge the privileges or immunities of citizens of the United States; nor shall any State deprive any person of life, liberty, or property, without due process of law; nor deny to any person within its jurisdiction the equal protection of the laws.

SECTION 2. Representatives shall be apportioned among the several States according to their respective numbers, counting the whole number of persons in each State, excluding Indians not taxed. But when the right to vote at any election for the choice of electors for President and Vice President of the United States, Representatives in Congress, the Executive and Judicial officers of a State, or the members of the Legislature thereof, is denied to any of the male inhabitants of such State, being twenty-one years of age, and citizens of the United States, or in any way abridged, except for participation in rebellion, or other crime, the basis of representation therein shall be reduced in the proportion which the number of such male citizens shall bear to the whole number of male citizens twenty one years of age in such State.

SECTION 3. No person shall be a Senator or Representative in Congress, or elector of President and Vice President, or hold any office, civil or military, under the United States, or under any State, who, having previously taken an oath, as a member of Congress, or as an officer of the United States, or as a member of any State legislature, or as an executive or judicial officer of any State, to support the Constitution of the United States, shall have engaged in insurrection or rebellion against the same, or given aid or comfort to the enemies thereof. But Congress may by a vote of two-thirds of each House, remove such disability.

or protections of any citizen of the United States. No State can take away any citizen's life, freedom, or belongings without proper use of the law. Every person is given the same protection under the law.

SECTION 2. Representatives will be figured among the States according to their numbers, counting all the people in the State, except Native Americans who are not taxed. If a State will not let any male citizen over 21 years old vote freely (unless he commits a crime, or takes part in a rebellion), the number of Representatives for that states will be reduced.

SECTION 3. No one can be a Senator, Representative, Elector or officer of the United States -- or United States military officer, or member of a State Legislature, or a Governor, or a judge of any State -- if they took an oath to support the Constitution and then took part in a rebellion against the United States, or gave aid and comfort to the enemies of the United States. But Congress can change this with a two-thirds vote.

SECTION 4. The validity of the public debt of the United States, authorized by law, including debts incurred for payment of pensions and bounties for services in suppressing insurrection or rebellion, shall not be questioned. But neither the United States nor any State shall assume or pay any debt or obligation incurred in aid of insurrection or rebellion against the United States, or any claim for the loss or emancipation of any slave; but all such debts, obligations and claims shall be held illegal and void.

SECTION 5. The Congress shall have power to enforce, by appropriate legislation, the provisions of this article.

AMENDMENT XV.

SECTION 1. The right of citizens of the United States to vote shall not be denied or abridged by the United States or by any State on account of race, color, or previous condition of servitude.

SECTION 2. The Congress shall have power to enforce this article by appropriate legislation.

AMENDMENT XVI

The Congress shall have power to lay and collect taxes on incomes, from whatever source derived, without apportionment among the several States, and without regard to any census or enumeration.

AMENDMENT XVII.

The Senate of the United States shall be composed of two Senators from each State, elected by the people thereof, for six years; and each Senator shall have one vote. The electors in each State shall have the qualifications requisite for electors of the most numer-

SECTION 4. Any money the United States owes for paying pensions, or pay for help in stopping a revolt, shall not be questioned. Neither the United States nor any State can pay any money for help in rebelling against the United States, and no State or the United States will pay for a lost or freed slave -- in fact all such bills, obligations, and claims are not legal.

SECTION 5. Congress has the power to enforce this amendment by law.

AMENDMENT 15 (February 3, 1868)

SECTION 1. The United States or any State cannot deny anyone the right to vote based on their race, the color of their skin, or the fact that they were once slaves.

SECTION 2. Congress has the power to enforce this amendment by law.

AMENDMENT 16 (February 3, 1913)

Congress has the power to place and collect taxes on citizens' incomes without regard to the States, or without counting people.

AMENDMENT [17] (April 8, 1913)

The Senate of the United States will be made up of two Senators from each State, elected by the people in that State, every six years. Each Senator will have one vote. The electors in each state have to have the same qualifications as electors of the biggest house of

ous branch of the State legislatures.

When vacancies happen in the representation of any State in the Senate, the executive authority of each State shall issue writs of election to fill such vacancies: Provided, That the legislature of any State may empower the executive thereof to make temporary appointments until the people fill the vacancies by election as the legislature may direct.

This amendment shall not be so construed as to affect the election or term of any Senator chosen before it becomes valid as part of the Constitution.

AMENDMENT XVIII.

SECTION 1. After one year from the ratification of this article the manufacture, sale, or transportation of intoxicating liquors within, the importation thereof into, or the exportation thereof from the United States and all territory subject to the jurisdiction thereof for beverage purposes is hereby prohibited.

SECTION 2. The Congress and the several States shall have concurrent power to enforce this article by appropriate legislation.

SECTION 3. This article shall be inoperative unless it shall have been ratified as an amendment to the Constitution by the legislatures of the several States, as provided in the Constitution, within seven years from the date of the submission hereof to the States by the Congress.]

AMENDMENT XIX.

The right of citizens of the United States to vote shall not be denied or abridged by the United States or by any State on account of sex.

Congress shall have power to enforce this article by appropriate legislation.

the State legislature (generally be registered to vote).

If a Senator dies or leaves office, the Governor of the State shall call for an election to elect a new Senator. The State Legislature can let the Governor appoint somebody to be the temporary Senator until that election is held.

This amendment will not change the election or term of any Senators until it becomes a valid part of the Constitution.

AMENDMENT 18 (January 16, 1919)

SECTION 1. One year after this amendment is official, nobody can make, sell, or move beer, wine, or liquor anywhere in the United States - or anywhere under the control of the United States.

(This Amendment was later repealed)

SECTION 2. Congress and the States have the power to enforce this amendment by law.

SECTION 3. This amendment will not work unless it is added to the Constitution by the State Legislatures, like the Constitution says, in seven years from the day it is given to the States by Congress.

AMENDMENT 19 (August 18, 1920)

Women can vote. The right to vote cannot be denied because of sex.

Congress can enforce this amendment by law.

AMENDMENT XX.

SECTION 1. The terms of the President and Vice President shall end at noon on the 20th day of January, and the terms of Senators and Representatives at noon on the 3rd day of January, of the years in which such terms would have ended if this article had not been ratified; and the terms of their successors shall then begin.

SECTION 2. The Congress shall assemble at least once in every year, and such meeting shall begin at noon on the 3rd day of January, unless they shall by law appoint a different day.

SECTION 3. If, at the time fixed for the beginning of the term of the President, the President elect shall have died, the Vice President elect shall become President. If a President shall not have been chosen before the time fixed for the beginning of his term, or if the President elect shall have failed to qualify, then the Vice President elect shall act as President until a President shall have qualified; and the Congress may by law provide for the case wherein neither a President elect nor a Vice President elect shall have qualified, declaring who shall then act as President, or the manner in which one who is to act shall be selected, and such person shall act accordingly until a President or Vice President shall have qualified.

SECTION 4. The Congress may by law provide for the case of the death of any of the persons from whom the House of Representatives may choose a President whenever the right of choice shall have devolved upon them, and for the case of the death of any of the persons from whom the Senate may choose a Vice President whenever the right of choice shall have devolved upon them.

AMENDMENT 20 (January 23, 1933)

SECTION 1. Terms of the President and the Vice-President end at noon on January 20th. Terms of Senators and Representatives will begin and end at noon on January 3rd. Terms of the new President and Vice President will begin at noon on January 20. Terms of new Senators and Representatives will begin at noon on January 3rd.

SECTION 2. Congress must meet at least once every year, starting on January 3rd, unless they pass a law to pick another day.

SECTION 3. If the President-elect dies after the election and before noon on January 20, the Vice President-Elect will become President. If, for some reason, a President is not chosen before January 20, or if the President-Elect does not meet the rules laid out in the Constitution, then the Vice President-Elect will act as President until someone is chosen as President.

If neither the President-Elect nor the Vice President-Elect meets the rules laid out in the Constitution, the Congress can decide, by law, who will act as President, how a President should then be picked, and that person will act as President until the Constitutional rules can be followed.

SECTION 4. If the Representatives ever have to choose a President, or the Senators ever have to choose a Vice President, and that person dies before they enter office, the Congress can make a law to deal with that.

·

SECTION 5. Sections 1 and 2 shall take effect on the 15th day of October following the ratification of this article.

SECTION 6. This article shall be inoperative unless it shall have been ratified as an amendment to the Constitution by the legislatures of three fourths of the several States within seven years from the date of its submission.

AMENDMENT XXI.

SECTION 1. The eighteenth article of amendment to the Constitution of the United States is hereby repealed.

SECTION 2. The transportation or importation into any State, Territory, or possession of the United States for delivery or use therein of intoxicating liquors, in violation of the laws thereof, is hereby prohibited.

SECTION 3. This article shall be inoperative unless it shall have been ratified as an amendment to the Constitution by conventions in the several States, as provided in the Constitution, within seven years from the date of the submission hereof to the States by the Congress.

AMENDMENT XXII.

SECTION 1. No person shall be elected to the office of the President more than twice, and no person who has held the office of President, or acted as President, for more than two years of a term to which some other person was elected President shall be elected to the office of President more than once. But this Article shall not apply to any person holding the office of President when this Article was proposed by the Congress, and shall not prevent any person who may be holding the office

SECTION 5. Section 1 and 2 will take effect on October 15 after this amendment becomes part of the Constitution.

SECTION 6. This amendment will not work unless it is added to the Constitution by the State Legislatures, like the Constitution says, seven years from the day after it is given to the States by Congress.

AMENDMENT 21 (Dec. 5, 1933)

SECTION 1. The eighteenth amendment is repealed.

SECTION 2. States, territories, or other areas under the control of the United States can still pass laws making it illegal to make, sell, move, or drink beer, wine, or liquor.

SECTION 3. This amendment will not work unless it is added to the Constitution by the State Legislatures, like the Constitution says, seven years from the day after it is given to the States by Congress.

AMENDMENT 22 (Feb. 27, 1951)

SECTION 1. Nobody can be elected President more than twice. Nobody who has held the office of President, or acted as President, for more than two years of someone else's term, can be elected more than once. This amendment does not affect the President now, and it does not affect anyone who may act as President until this amendment is officially added to the Constitution.

of President, or acting as President, during the term within which this Article becomes operative from holding the office of President or acting as President during the remainder of such term.

SECTION 2. This article shall be inoperative unless it shall have been ratified as an amendment to the Constitution by the legislatures of three-fourths of the several States within seven years from the date of its submission to the States by the Congress.

SECTION 2. This amendment will not work unless it is added to the Constitution by the State Legislatures, like the Constitution says, seven years from the day after it is given to the States by Congress.

AMENDMENT XXIII.

AMENDMENT 23 (March 29, 1961)

SECTION 1. The District constituting the seat of Government of the United States shall appoint in such manner as the Congress may direct:

SECTION 1. The place where the seat of government is located (Washington, the District of Columbia) can pick Electors like this:

A number of electors of President and Vice President equal to the whole number of Senators and Representatives in Congress to which the District would be entitled if it were a State, but in no event more than the least populous State; they shall be in addition to those appointed by the States, but they shall be considered, for the purposes of the election of President and Vice President, to be electors appointed by a State; and they shall meet in the District and perform such duties as provided by the twelfth article of amendment.

The number of Electors will be figured as if the District of Columbia were a State, and the number would equal the number of Senators and Representatives of the smallest State. These Electors would be in addition to the Electors chosen by the States. For the election of the President and Vice President, the Electors will act like they are from a State. They will meet in the District of Columbia and follow the rules of the 12th amendment.

SECTION 2. The Congress shall have the power to enforce this article by appropriate legislation.

SECTION 2. Congress has the power to enforce this amendment by law.

AMENDMENT XXIV.

AMENDMENT 24 (January 23, 1964)

SECTION 1. The right of citizens of the United States to vote in any primary or other election for President or Vice President, for electors for President or Vice President, or for

SECTION 1. No state can make people pay a tax as a condition of voting in any election for President, Senator or Representative.

47

Senator or Representative in Congress, shall not be denied or abridged by the United States or any State by reason of failure to pay any poll tax or other tax.

SECTION 2. The Congress shall have the power to enforce this article by appropriate legislation.

SECTION 2. Congress has the power to enforce this amendment by law.

AMENDMENT XXV.

AMENDMENT 25 (Feb. 10, 1967)

SECTION 1. In case of the removal of the President from office or of his death or resignation, the Vice President shall become President.

SECTION 1. If the President dies, leaves office, or gets kicked out of office (impeached), the Vice President becomes the President.

SECTION 2. Whenever there is a vacancy in the office of the Vice President, the President shall nominate a Vice President who shall take office upon confirmation by a majority vote of both Houses of Congress.

SECTION 2. If there is not a Vice President, the President will pick one, and that person will be the Vice President after a majority of Senators and Representatives allow it.

SECTION 3. Whenever the President transmits to the President pro tempore of the Senate and the Speaker of the House of Representatives his written declaration that he is unable to discharge the powers and duties of his office, and until he transmits to them a written declaration to the contrary, such powers and duties shall be discharged by the Vice President as Acting President.

SECTION 3. If the President writes to the President of the Senate and the Speaker of the House of Representatives and tells them the President can no longer do the job -- the Vice President will become the Acting President. The President who gave up the office would have to write to the President of the Senate and the Speaker of the House again to let them know she or he can do the job again.

SECTION 4. Whenever the Vice President and a majority of either the principal officers of the executive departments or of such other body as Congress may by law provide, transmit to the President pro tempore of the Senate and the Speaker of the House of Representatives their written declaration that the President is unable to discharge the power and duties of his office, the Vice President shall immediately assume the powers and duties of the office as Acting President.

SECTION 4. If the Vice President and a majority of the Cabinet officers writes to the President of the Senate and the Speaker of the House to tell them the President cannot do the job, the Vice President will immediately begin acting as President.

Thereafter, when the President transmits to the President pro tempore of the Senate and the Speaker of the House of Representatives his written declaration that no inability exists, he shall resume the powers and duties of his office unless the Vice President and a majority of either the principal officers of the executive department or of such other body as Congress may by law provide, transmit within four days to the President pro tempore of the Senate and the Speaker of the House of Representatives their written declaration that the President is unable to discharge the powers and duties of his office. Thereupon Congress shall decide the issue, assembling within forty-eight hours for that purpose if not in session. If the Congress, within twenty-one days after receipt of the latter written declaration, or, if Congress is not in session, within twenty-one days after Congress is required to assemble, determines by two-thirds vote of both Houses that the President is unable to discharge the powers and duties of his office, the Vice President shall continue to discharge the same as Acting President; otherwise, the President shall resume the powers and duties of his office.

AMENDMENT XXVI.

SECTION 1. The right of citizens of the United States, who are eighteen years of age or older, to vote shall not be denied or abridged by the United States or by any State on account of age.

Sec. 2. The Congress shall have the power to enforce this article by appropriate legislation.

AMENDMENT XXVII.

(Article the Second . . .) No law, varying the compensation for the services of the Senators and Representatives, shall take effect, until an election of Representatives shall have intervened.

After that, when the original President writes to the President of the Senate and the Speaker of the House to tell them she or he can now do the job, the President will again have the powers of office -- unless the Vice President and a majority of the Cabinet officers write the President of the Senate and the Speaker of the House within four days to tell them that is not the case. If all that happens, Congress will meet within 48 hours to decide the issue. Congress must act within 21 days of receiving the letter. If Senators and Representatives decide by a two-thirds vote that the original President cannot do the job, the Vice President will continue to act as President. Otherwise, the President gets back the power of office.

AMENDMENT 26 (July 1, 1971)

SECTION 1. Citizens who are 18 years old may now vote. The United States or any State cannot deny anyone the right to vote based on age.

Sec. 2. Congress has the power to enforce this amendment by law.

AMENDMENT 27 (May 18, 1992)

Congress cannot get a raise unless an election happens since they passed the law giving themselves a raise.

Since the Constitution was written ...

Since the Founders wrote the Constitution so long ago, Congress has passed a bunch of laws about nearly everything.

We selected our 43rd President in 2000. Some presidents have been pretty good; others have been average. President Abraham Lincoln kept the states together as a country during and after the Civil War. President John F. Kennedy kept the nation out of a nuclear war in 1962. But the enduring magic of our government is that power is surrendered peacefully after our elections.

The 21st Century brought us our 107th Congress, and Congress is always in an argument with the President to see who has the most power. It is the job of Congress to spend the money that people pay to support the government. The President can tell Congress how he or she wants to spend the money, but Congress has the final say.

Our most basic political struggle continues to be about the power of the federal government and the power of the states ... that was true when the country was born, it was true at our worst moment (the Civil War), and it is true today. The Civil War tragically divided us on that question, and the federal government won. But the power of the states was apparent in the success southern states had keeping African Americans from voting from 1865 until 1965, exactly one hundred years after the Civil War was over.

The Supreme Court has made a bunch of decisions in arguments between citizens, states, and the government of the United States. Some of today's laws come from decisions that the Supreme Court made over the last 200 years. Although the Constitution has always said all citizens were equal, the Court finally began deciding some cases about 50 years ago that began to treat all people equally.

People are always going to disagree with the government, just because they have a right to do that. That is a very precious right, and we must always protect it and exercise it. People in this country can say just about anything they want, about anything or anybody they want, and they are protected by the First Amendment. They may not be right, they may not be nice, they may not even make any sense, but they can always say what they wish.

To be part of our history, remember what is in the Constitution and make sure that your rights and liberties are exercised and protected, as well as those of your family and friends. The Constitution governs everyone who lives in the United States, not just the adults. It only works when people know what it means.

Use the information in <u>Constitution Translated for Kids</u> to know what to expect of your government right now, and to understand the liberties and responsibilities of living in the United States of America.

Words to look at while you are reading:

(This list does not include all the hard words in the original text of the Constitution, only in the translation.)

Amended - If a law is amended, that means we just added more to it, or made it different.

Appointed - In the United States, people who get picked by a President to serve in the government or on the courts, are appointed.

Bail - Money people pay to get out of jail while they wait on their trial.

Ballot - A ballot is a little piece of paper on which people write down their votes (most people cast electronic ballots now). Presidential electors still use paper ballots (which are Constitutionally mandated).

Bill, Act, Law - If someone in Congress has an idea for a law, they write it down for everybody to read and it is called a "bill," or an "act." After a bill has been passed by Congress and signed by the President, it is the law.

Cabinet - The Cabinet is made up of people the President picks to be in charge of the different departments in the government. In the United States, the people in the President's Cabinet are his or her official advisors.

Candidate - A candidate is somebody who runs for office.

Case - When people are accused of a crime and they have to go to court, they are part of a case. The case is what the people, and the person blamed for the crime, tell the judge and the jury.

Census - The Census is the official count of people in the country; we take it every 10 years.

Citizen, Citizenship - If you were born in a country, you are a citizen of that country. Citizenship is what you have if you are a citizen. If you weren't born in the United States, you have to live in the U.S. for a while and take a test before you can be a citizen, unless your parents are both citizens.

Constitution - The word itself actually means to set things up and get things started. In the United States, the Constitution got the United States government all set up.

Delegation - A delegation is a group of people that officially represents other people.

Democracy - Democracy is a form of government where all the people in the country can vote for the people who make the laws.

Elections, elected - Elections are when people vote for their leaders. The candidates with the most votes are elected. In presidential races, the person with the most electoral votes wins the office.

Elector, Electoral College - An Elector is one of a few people in a state who vote for the President. When people vote for President and Vice President they are actually voting for electors. The Electoral College is the group of people from all the states that cast votes for the President and Vice-President. The Electoral College only exists once every 4 years.

Empower - Empower means to give someone legal power.

Enforce - Enforce means to make someone mind and follow the rules.

Federal - The United States has several levels of government. There are local governments (cities and towns); there are state governments; and there is the federal government. The federal government is what the Constitution set up, in the federal city, Washington, D.C.

Founders - Founders are people who get a country or a movement started. In the United States, the Founders were a group of men whose families had come from Europe, and who wanted to start their own country.

Governor - In the United States, a governor is the top person in charge of a State.

Grand Jury - This is a small group of people gathered by the local authorities to decide if there is enough evidence to try someone for a crime.

Impeach, Impeachment - The word "impeach" actually means to discredit. In the United States government, impeaching someone is the first part of the process to kick people out of office. If someone is "impeached" he or she is accused by the House of Representatives, and the Senate can then hold the "impeachment trial" to either kick him or her out of office or decide that he or she do not deserve to get kicked out. The House acts as a grand jury and the Senate as jury for impeachment cases.

Income - Income is the money that people make from working.

Journal - A Journal is sort of like a diary. It is the official record of daily meetings in Congress.

Judge(s) - A Judge is a person who hears cases in court. The judges are always in charge in a courtroom, and they give directions to the people talking and to the jury that decides the case.

Jury - A jury is a group of 12 people who don't know the person on trial, and who settle arguments between people in a case in court.

Legislature - The legislature is the elected group of people who make laws. In the United States, each state has a legislature. The country's legislature is the Congress.

Officers - An officer is someone who holds an office of trust in the civilian government. Officers are also people in the military who are in charge of other military people.

Override - When Congress votes with two-thirds of the members present, they can override a President's veto of a law Congress passed. If Congress is successful in their "veto override," the bill in question becomes law anyway.

Quorum - A quorum is the least amount of people needed to do business in Congress.

Ratify, Ratified - To formally approve, to give legal power, is to ratify something.

Repealed - If a law is repealed, it is completely erased.

Supreme - "Supreme" means highest. The Supreme Court is the highest court in the land. The supreme law of the United States is the Constitution, no law is more powerful; it is the highest law in the nation.

Tax, Taxed - A tax is money that people pay to support the government. People who make money legally are "taxed."

Treason, Crimes - Crimes are behaviors that break the law. Treason is a really bad crime, because it is a crime against everybody in the country. The Constitution lays out a real clear explanation of treason (Article 3, Section 3).

Trial, Try - A trial is the courtroom contest between the person blamed for the crime and the accusers, in front of the judge and jury. To "try" somebody means to have a trial.

Veto - The word itself means to forbid, a veto is an official act that forbids something. In the Constitution, if the President opposes a law passed by Congress, it is vetoed.

Warrant - Warrants are what judges give police if they think someone is breaking the law - it allows police to search private homes or arrest somebody.

A Workbook for Constitution Translated for Kids

Just reading the Constitution may not help you remember it later. But answering questions about it, talking about it, and understanding how it works for you might help you remember it better.

When you talk about it, try to think about examples of how it could apply to you, or to your family, and your state.

GENERAL OVERVIEW

Who does the Constitution belong to, and who does it govern?

The Constitution sets up the U.S. government. How many branches of government do we have? List them.

How many Articles does the Constitution have?

How many amendments?

CONGRESS:

Congress consists of two Houses (or two parts) - what are they?

Which part of Congress has the most members? Why?

Is there still one representative for every 30,000 people?

How many Senators are there? How many per state?

Who serves as President of the Senate?

Who is the top officer for the House of Representatives?

Can the House of Representatives or the Senate leave (adjourn) while the other one is still meeting? (Adjourn means to finish the legislative business and dismiss the members.)

Bills that raise money (taxes) ALWAYS begin where?

There are two ways for a bill to become a law; what are they?

Congress generally makes laws, but what are some of the specific powers the Constitution gives to Congress?

How old do you have to be to serve in the House? In the Senate?

EXECUTIVE BRANCH (PRESIDENCY)

Who is the one person who is ultimately in charge of the country?

When people vote for president, they aren't really voting for a person running for president; who do they vote for?

What are electors?

If something happens to the President, who becomes the next President?

If somebody was born in another country, and moved here when he or she were still a baby, could he or she still grow up to be President? Why, why not?

Besides generally running the country, what other responsibilities does the Constitution give the President?

If a President gets impeached by the House of Representatives, does the President have to leave office?

Why would the Constitution give some pretty important responsibilities to the President, but also make some of them subject to the "advice and consent (permission)" of the Senate?

Our Founders established a system of "checks and balances" so one person could not undermine the good of the whole country. What are some examples?

Why do you think the Constitution insists that if Congress overrides a veto, they must do so with two-thirds of their members?

JUDICIARY

How long can a Justice (Supreme or Federal Court Judge) serve?

What is the main thing the Supreme Court does?

How does the Constitution define treason (the act of a traitor)?

STATES

The Founders wanted the States to have a good deal of power. Each State has to honor the other states' acts, records and legal reports. Who judges these records and laws in case they conflict?

If somebody commits a crime in one state, can they just go to another state and forget about it?

How can new states join the United States?

Can states leave the United States after they join?

HOUSEKEEPING

Is the Constitution finished? Can we add something to it? If so, how?

What is considered the "supreme law of the land?"

How do we bind elected or appointed officers of our government to support the Constitution?

What religious test must people pass to serve in office?

AMENDMENTS:

The first 10 amendments to the Constitution speak to individual liberties for each person who lives in the country. What are the first 10 amendments generally called?

1st Amendment: Individual freedoms

What are the individual freedoms listed in the 1st Amendment?

According to the Constitution, how do we pick religions or how to worship - or not worship - God?

What if a TV reporter or a newspaper says something untrue about someone or something very important and scares everybody?

If people can say anything, anywhere, anytime ... can you yell "fire" in a crowded theater ... or "shark" on a crowded beach ... or "bomb" at your school?

People are free to assemble freely. Can a bunch of people assemble in the middle of a busy highway?

If a million people asked Congress to change something or do something that Congress didn't want to do, can Congress make people stop asking?

2nd Amendment: Gun ownership as foundation for militias

When the U.S. was formed, the Founders were very concerned about the possibility of another war. Citizen soldiers played a pivotal role in the American Revolution, and to be ready for another war, the Founders wanted to make sure we could always preserve a citizen militia.

Can Congress make laws to regulate guns?

How come everybody says there is a Constitutional right to own a gun?

3rd Amendment: Housing of soldiers

Has there ever been a time when soldiers stayed in people's homes?

There's a soldier in my family; can he or she stay in my house?

4th Amendment: Search and arrest warrants for property and people

My mother is always coming in my room and going through my things. Does she have a right to do that?

5th Amendment: Rights of individuals in criminal cases

What are the rights the 5th Amendment gives citizens accused of crimes?

What if somebody was tried and found guilty for killing somebody, but he really didn't do it.... then to get even, he actually did kill the person he were supposed to have killed. Can he be tried again?

What if somebody was tried for a crime, but was found innocent, then wrote a book saying he did it, could he be tried again?

What does it mean when someone "takes the fifth?"

If the Army wanted to build an Army base on land my family owns, can they just do it?

What if they wanted to build a road?

6th Amendment: Rights for a fair trial

This Amendment is the basis for the idea of justice in our courts and systems of courts, that criminal justice should be guided by the fact that people are "innocent until proven guilty."

What are the criminal protections the Constitution offers citizens?

Can police make up stuff and arrest people?

What if the person on trial can't find any witnesses to tell the court his or her side of the story?

7th Amendment: Rights in civil cases

The Founders thought that trial by jury was real important to a democracy, and they made sure in the 6th Amendment that people had a jury for criminal trials, and the 7th Amendment makes sure they have one for civil trials in excess of $20 in federal court. There are two kinds of civil punishments: money or an injunction (an injunction is an order to make somebody do something or stop doing something).

Since $20 means something entirely different today than it did when they wrote the Constitution, nearly all civil cases have a jury now.

What's the difference between criminal trials and civil trials?

8th Amendment: Bails, fines, punishments

If somebody poor commits a crime, what's a reasonable fine or bail for them?

What if somebody really rich commits a crime, can pay the "reasonable" bail, but everybody figures he/she will just leave before the trial?

How can a punishment be kind, or not cruel and unusual?

9th Amendment: Rights retained by the people

The Constitution stipulates that the document cannot deny or abuse other rights of the people.

Why were the Founders worried that what they had written could be used against people?

10th Amendment: Powers retained by the states and the people

Were the Founders worried that the Bill of Rights would be interpreted in a way that could deprive people of their rights?

But the 9th Amendment made it clear that the Constitution couldn't be used against anyone, why the need for the 10th Amendment?

11th Amendment: Lawsuits against states

This amendment kept citizens of one state from suing another state in the federal courts. It came about when a man from one state sued another state over an inheritance. When the Supreme Court decided that states could be sued, this amendment was passed to clarify the legal powers of the Supreme Court. But people can still sue state officials in federal courts, so the effect is not that great.

If I felt I was wronged by another state, could I sue that state?

12th Amendment: Election of the President and Vice President

NOTE: There is also a federal law that goes into more detail about how this operates. These questions are only about what is in the Constitution.

What is an elector?

How do electors get picked?

How many electors does each state get?

What are electors generally called today when they meet to elect the President and Vice President?

How do electors elect the President and Vice President?

What happens when the electoral votes get to Washington?

What if nobody gets a majority?

What happens if the Representatives fool around and do not make a decision at all? Who is the president then?

Who picks the Vice President? How?

Has the House of Representatives ever had to choose the President before in a "contingent election?"

Why do we still pick the President this way? Why can't people just vote for a presidential ticket directly?

Is it possible for the person who got the most votes in the election to lose the vote in the Electoral College?

13th Amendment: Abolishment of slavery

Why did we have to include an amendment actually abolishing slavery when we fought the Civil War over that question?

Was it really necessary to write down that slavery didn't exist anymore? Isn't it enough that Congress could pass a law about it?

What about prisoners who get locked up? Is that considered slavery?

14th Amendment: Equal protection under the law for everyone

The most fundamental thing this amendment put in the Constitution was the concept of equal protection under the law for every person living in the United States. It also emphasized that anyone born in the United States was a citizen, entitled to the liberties of citizens.

Weren't people who lived here already, even if they were slaves once, already citizens? The Constitution even originally counted them in the population, although they were counted as three-fifths of a person.

What if states still did not want to let some people, like former slaves or their children, vote?

If somebody owned a slave, and the slave was freed by the 13th Amendment, could he get a refund?

Does it deny anything?

15th Amendment: Voting rights

If the 14th Amendment offered equal protection under the law for all citizens, why would we need an amendment saying former slaves could vote?

16th Amendment: Congress' power to tax

Is it fairer for Congress to get money this way, or the original way, where taxes were determined by the population?

Why did they need to change it?

17th Amendment: Direct election of U.S. Senators

How come it took so long for us to actually vote for our Senators?

How many Senators does each state get?

How long do they serve?

How many votes does each Senator get?

What happens if a Senator dies while in office or leaves office?

18th Amendment - Prohibition of alcohol

Why in the world did they think we needed a Constitutional Amendment to get rid of alcohol?

So, how come we still sell alcohol?

19th Amendment - Women get the right to vote

How come women didn't vote from the beginning of the country?

20th Amendment - Terms of service for the President, Vice President, and Congress

When do the terms of the President and the Vice-President begin and end?

When do the terms of Congress (Senators and Representatives) begin and end?

How often does Congress have to meet?

What if the new President (called a President-elect) dies after he gets elected, but before January 20, when he is officially the country's president?

What if something gets really messed up and the President-elect cannot act as President?

What happens if the House of Representatives has to choose a President and the person they pick dies before they enter office?

21st Amendment: Repeal of 18th Amendment

Are there any other amendments that got repealed (cancelled)?

How come it got repealed?

22nd Amendment: Limit of Presidential terms

How come we limit the terms a President can serve? Since we vote for them (or for their electors), if they do a bad job, can't we just vote them out?

How many terms can a President serve?

What if a President dies, and the Vice President serves out the term of office for the President, can that new President still be elected to two terms?

23rd Amendment: Washington, D.C. electors for President

How many Presidential electors does Washington, D.C. get?

How come they don't have electors based on representation like all the other states?

Do people in Washington DC have to pay taxes like everybody else?

24th Amendment: Elimination of the poll tax

What is a poll tax exactly?

How did the poll tax get started?

How come we eliminated it?

25th Amendment: Succession of office

What happens if the President dies, leaves office or gets impeached?

What if there is not a Vice President, for whatever reason, if they die or something?

Suppose the President gets shot or hurt or something happens to him/her? What happens then?

Is the President the only one who can say that she/he is not able to do the job?

26th Amendment: Right of 18 year-old citizens to vote

How come the Congress decided to lower the age requirements for voting?

27th Amendment: Determination of Congressional pay raises

How does Congress give themselves a raise?

What made this such an important issue that they made it a Constitutional Amendment?

THAT IS THE END OF THE CONSTITUTION AS IT NOW EXISTS.

Student Exercise in Democracy

If you had the chance to add to the United States Constitution now, or in the next few years, to improve or perfect our democracy, what would you want to add?

Since the Constitution is not finished, what are some other ideas for amendments to the Constitution? Debate them to understand why some things are just too hard to get agreement by two-thirds of any group.

Remember that the Constitution has only been amended 27 times in over 200 years, so an amendment should be extraordinarily necessary to make it part of the Constitution. Also remember that the Founders gave Congress the ability to make laws to deal with anything they saw fit, so just about any issue people want to add to the Constitution can be dealt with by passing a law.

In every debate about a new amendment, the most important question is: how vital is this that it must be added to the Constitution, or can Congress or local governments just make a law or a rule to deal with this issue?

Assume your group has succeeded in convening a constitutional convention. Below are suggestions for amendments, along with a suggestion or two to consider as arguments for and against the various amendments. Don't limit anyone's imagination by only using these suggestions or by sticking strictly to the way it is written.

If you can get two-thirds of any group to support any of these amendments, remember the actual process of adopting an amendment to the United States Constitution would also require that the amendment be adopted by two-thirds of the United States Congress and three-fourths of the states as well.

Incidently, many of these amendments are actually proposed by someone in Congress or the states to amend the Constitution.

PROPOSED AMENDMENT:

The Balanced Budget Amendment

WHAT IT IS:

This amendment requires the government of the United States to balance the budget of the United States every single year from now on.

POINTS TO DISCUSS FOR THE AMENDMENT:

* The United States should never spend more money than it takes in; that just makes good sense.

* Families have to balance their budgets, so why can't the government?

POINTS TO DISCUSS AGAINST THE AMENDMENT:

* What if the United States goes to war, or has a national emergency like a hurricane or floods, or something that would require us to spend more money than we have right then to further the national cause?

* Most families carry some sort of debt, either a mortgage on their house, a car note or some credit card bills.

PROPOSED AMENDMENT:

Protection of the United States flag

WHAT IT IS:

Burning the American flag will never be permitted and anyone who does that will be punished to the fullest extent of the law.

POINTS TO DISCUSS FOR THE AMENDMENTT:

* The flag is the symbol of the country, and burning it diminishes the nation.

* People who burn the flag are traitors and deserve punishment for disrespecting the flag.

* Our flag flies over people who fight for our nation, burning it demeans their effort.

POINTS TO DISCUSS AGAINST THE AMENDMENT :

* The Constitution is the foundation of the country and the flag, while inspirational, is only a piece of cloth.

* The Constitution lays out a real clear definition of what treason is: to aid and comfort enemies. Burning a flag doesn't comfort an enemy, more likely it would just confuse them.

* There is not currently a problem with lots of people burning flags. Why amend the Constitution to tend to a problem that doesn't exist?

PROPOSED AMENDMENT:

Campaign finance amendment

WHAT IT IS:

All candidates for federal elected office must accept limits on the amount of money they can spend on campaigns for office. Congress, along with the states, gets to decide what that limit is and how candidates can get money for campaigns.

POINTS TO DISCUSS FOR THE AMENDMENT:

* Far too much money is collected by candidates for federal office each year, largely from corporations and businesses - organizations that will be governed by the rules made by the Congress and the President.

* Democracy is hurt when money has more influence on elections than voters.

POINTS TO DISCUSS AGAINST THE AMENDMENT:

* Everybody in our democracy, including companies and businesses, should be able to participate in elections, to whatever extent they choose.

* Our laws have never been more strict on how candidates can collect and spend money. It does not need to be, and should not be, part of the Constitution.

PROPOSED AMENDMENT:

Repeal the 16th Amendment

WHAT IT IS:

This will repeal the 16th Amendment, allowing Congress to again collect taxes based on population, or in another manner they choose (other than on the income of individuals or companies).

POINTS TO DISCUSS FOR THE AMENDMENT:

* Taxing people based on their incomes is unfair because someone who works harder to make more money shouldn't have to pay more taxes.

* Our Founders wanted the federal government to be very small. Taxing by income goes against that logic.

POINTS TO DISCUSS AGAINST THE AMENDMENT:

* Congress must raise money to do its job. Taxing citizens by income is the best way for Congress to get money to run the country, defend the nation, and meet all our financial obligations.

* Changing how we pay our bills is enormously difficult to figure. If we do this, whoever supports the amendment will have to decide a new way to pay our bills, which can run about $2 trillion annually.

PROPOSED AMENDMENT:

The Victims' Rights Amendment

WHAT IT IS:

This amendment will give the victim of crimes, or the family of the victim of crimes, the ability to be heard in the court during the trial of the accused and to be heard before sentencing of a criminal.

POINTS TO DISCUSS FOR THE AMENDMENT:

* Criminals have too many protections from the Bill of Rights, but the victims of crimes have no rights, and no voice in the court-room

POINTS TO DISCUSS AGAINST THE AMENDMENT:

* Victims of crimes or their families are not on trial for their lives, or for any part of their lives. They don't need the rights or protections we give people accused of crimes.

PROPOSED AMENDMENT:

Lowering voting age to 16

WHAT IT IS:

This amendment will offer the right to vote to 16 year-old citizens.

POINTS TO DISCUSS FOR THE AMENDMENT:

* People mature earlier now, and 16 year-old people are better educated and should have the opportunity to vote for people who are making decisions on their behalf.

* Some 16 year-olds work and pay taxes.

POINTS TO DISCUSS AGAINST THE AMENDMENT:

* Most 16 year-olds are not that mature and haven't even gotten out of high school yet. We should be very careful how young our electorate may get.

* The age of 18 is generally the age of reason in our laws. The consent to marry, to make health-related decisions, and to be drafted for war begins at age 18.

PROPOSED AMENDMENT:

Prohibition of tobacco

WHAT IT IS:

This amendment will make the growing, possession or selling of tobacco illegal in every U.S. state and territory.

POINTS TO DISCUSS FOR THE AMENDMENT:

* We abolished alcohol once, so this has been done.

* Doctors have been telling us for years that tobacco is deadly; this is not just a bad habit, it is killing people, and costing us billions of dollars in health care costs.

POINTS TO DISCUSS AGAINST THE AMENDMENT:

* The best evidence against this amendment is the existence of the 21st Amendment.

* Attempts to prohibit tobacco will only make it more expensive and jail tobacco farmers and smokers.

PROPOSED AMENDMENT:

Prohibition of the death penalty

WHAT IT IS:

Any criminal convicted in a state or federal court can no longer be assigned to die for their crime or crimes.

POINTS TO DISCUSS FOR THE AMENDMENT:

* The Bill of Rights says a punishment cannot be cruel or unusual; surely killing someone is cruel and unusual.

* In the 10 most basic laws for Jews and Christians (the 10 Commandments), it is clear that "Thou shalt not kill."

POINTS TO DISCUSS AGAINST THE AMENDMENT:

* The death penalty would keep that criminal from ever committing a crime again, and show other criminals what will happen to them.

* The Bible also says, "An eye for an eye, a tooth for a tooth" so if we follow that to a conclusion, if somebody kills somebody, it is OK to kill them.

What other ideas do you have for proposed amendments to the Constitution?

THE MATH OF A PRESIDENTIAL CAMPAIGN:

Since we now have a better idea of how presidential candidates get elected, see which states you think are the most important to visit in order to get the 270 electoral votes to win a presidential election.

Here is how many votes each state has in the Electoral College in 2004:

Alabama,9	Kentucky, 8	North Dakota, 3
Alaska, 3	Louisiana, 9	Ohio, 20
Arizona, 10	Maine, 4	Oklahoma, 7
Arkansas, 6	Maryland, 10	Oregon, 7
California, 55	Massachusetts, 12	Pennsylvania, 21
Colorado, 9	Michigan, 17	Rhode Island, 4
Connecticut, 7	Minnesota, 10	South Carolina, 8
Delaware, 3	Mississippi, 6	South Dakota, 3
District of Columbia, 3	Missouri, 11	Tennessee, 11
Florida, 27	Montana, 3	Texas, 34
Georgia, 15	Nebraska, 5	Utah, 5
Hawaii, 4	Nevada, 5	Vermont, 3
Idaho, 4	New Hampshire, 4	Virginia, 13
Illinois, 21	New Jersey, 15	Washington, 11
Indiana, 11	New Mexico, 5	West Virginia, 5
Iowa, 7	New York, 31	Wisconsin, 10
Kansas, 6	North Carolina, 15	Wyoming, 3

The top 11 most populous states in the country (California, Florida, Georgia, Illinois, Michigan, New Jersey, New York, North Carolina, Ohio, Pennsylvania and Texas) control how many electoral votes?

The next tier of states, those that have 10 electoral votes or more (Arizona, Indiana, Maryland, Massachusetts, Minnesota, Missouri, Tennessee, Virginia, Washington and Wisconsin), control how many electoral votes?

The remaining 29 states, each having less than 10 electoral votes apiece, control how many electoral votes among them?

Some of the top 10 or 11 states are usually loyal to one political party or the other, so candidates mark those accordingly, then decide on a strategy of putting together a majority of 270 electoral votes from the states on the next tier of electoral states (those with at least 10 votes) or some of the other 29 states.

How many electoral votes does your state have?

If you were working for a presidential campaign, or if you were running for president, which states would you try the hardest to win to get the 270 votes needed to win the electoral college?

Do you think the Electoral College is still a useful way to elect a president?

Or should we elect a president like we elect Representatives, Senators and other people who serve in public office (through direct elections, whoever gets the most votes wins)?

What are the chances we would elect a president through direct elections, whoever gets the most votes wins?

WHAT CONSTITUTIONAL PRIVILEGE DO THESE THINGS VIOLATE?

Choose which individual liberties, guaranteed by the Bill of Rights, that the following actions would violate. (And some may violate none at all.)

* Somebody stands across the street from the police station, not interrupting anybody's work. This person gives a speech for the whole day about how the police are using tactics that are illegal, and the person making the speech gets arrested.

* Somebody gets arrested, but the police don't tell him/her the reason for the arrest.

* People sent a petition to Congress asking them to fix something and Congress doesn't do it.

* Congress passed a law forbidding a "Keepers of the Faith" religion (or they pass a law that prohibited ANY religion).

* Army commanders required area homeowners to let soldiers stay at their house when there was a housing shortage.

* Congress passed a law saying people couldn't pray in public.

* Congress passed a law keeping people from buying a certain kind of gun.

* A Judge makes the person on trial tell why they broke the law.

* A person on trial was not told why they were being arrested.

* The government shut down a newspaper because they wrote something that was really wrong about something important (but they didn't mean to, they were just bad at their job).

* The Ku Klux Klan is denied a permit to gather in a town to stage a peaceful protest.

BIBLIOGRAPHY:

Commission on the Bicentennial of the United States Constitution (1992) The Constitution of the United States, Eighteenth Edition (with 27th Amendment). Washington, D.C., Government Printing Office.

Simendinger, A., Barnes, J.A., & Cannon, C.M. (November 18, 2000) "After the Great Close Call," National Journal. Washington, D.C., National Journal Group, Inc.

Peirce, N. & Longley, L.D. (1981) The People's President. New Haven, CT, Yale University Press.

Dellinger, W. (1993) "The Legitimacy of Constitutional Change: Rethinking the Amendment Process," Harvard Law Review. Boston, MA, Harvard University Press.

United States House of Representatives (1992) The Constitution of the United States of American As Amended, H. Doc. No. 102-188, 102nd Congress, 2nd Session. Washington, D.C., Government Printing Office.

Venetoulis, T.G. (1968) The House Shall Choose. Margate, NJ, Elias Press.

United States Senate Committee on the Judiciary (1932) Report to Accompany S.J. Res. 14, 72nd Congress, 1st Session. Washington, D.C., Government Printing Office.

Congressional Research Service (1997) The Constitution of the United States, Analysis and Interpretation, 1996 Supplement. Washington, D.C., Government Printing Office.

U.S. Electoral College: List Of States And Votes: 2004, Allocation of Electoral Votes based on the 2000 Census. National Archives and Records Administration, Federal Register web site: http://www.nara.gov/fedreg/elctcoll/vote2004 .

FindLaw International Legal Resources, web site: http://supreme.lp.findlaw.com/

Special thanks to the following friends:

Ms. Silvia Golombek, PhD
Ms. Nancy Bacot
Mr. Lawrence L. Calvert, Jr., Esquire
Ms. Darlene DenHollander, Esquire
Ms. Clara Pizaña
Mr. Chris Robicheux
Mr. Bill Miles
Ms. Gail Bomer

Actual image of U.S. Constitution, as ratified September 17, 1789.

Article II.

Article III.

Article IV.

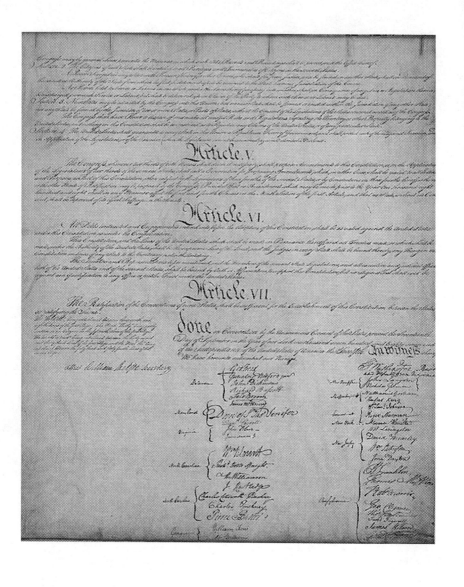